SAN FRANCISCO
THEN & NOW

Thunder Bay Press
An imprint of the Advantage Publishers Group
5880 Oberlin Drive, San Diego, CA 92121-4794
www.thunderbaybooks.com

Produced by Salamander Books,
an imprint of Anova Books Company Ltd.,
151 Freston Road, London W10 6TH, United Kingdom

All notations of errors or omissions should be addressed to Thunder Bay Press,
Editorial Department, at the above address. All other correspondence (author
inquiries, permissions) concerning the content of this book should be addressed to
Salamander Books, 151 Freston Road, London, W10 6TH, U.K.

ISBN-13: 978-1-59223-730-2
ISBN-10: 1-59223-730-4

The Library of Congress has cataloged the original Thunder Bay edition as follows:
Yenne, Bill, 1949–
San Francisco then & now / Bill Yenne.
    p. cm.
Includes index
ISBN 1-57145-156-0
1. San Francisco (Calif.)--Pictorial works. 2. San Francisco
(Calif.)--History--Pictorial works. I. Title
F889.S343Y46 1998
979.4'61--dc21   98-33603
                                        CIP

1 2 3 4 5 11 10 09 08 07

Printed in China

PHOTO CREDITS

All photographs on left hand (even numbered) pages are courtesy of the San Francisco Archives, with the
following exceptions:
Clo Kennedy: 40
National Archives: 20, 70, 90, 112
Noe Valley Archives: 122 (both), 126, 128, 130, 132, 134
Jane Perry: 136
Personal collection of the author: 16, 24, 26, 30, 32, 36 (both), 40, 46, 48, 68, 72, 74, 78, 102, 114, 126,
128, 142 (both)
Western History Center: 6, 18, 53, 56, 76, 80, 94, 110
US Army: 58
US Navy: 82
© Bill Yenne: 2

All photographs on right hand (odd numbered) pages are by and copyright © Bill Yenne, with the
following exceptions:
California Department of Transportation: 1
Personal collection of the author: 25, 29
© Azia Yenne: 73

SAN FRANCISCO
THEN & NOW

BILL YENNE

THUNDER BAY
P·R·E·S·S

San Diego, California

INTRODUCTION

SAN FRANCISCO IS MANY THINGS TO MANY PEOPLE. The popular slogan calls it "Everybody's Favorite City," an appellation confirmed year after year as *Condé Nast Traveler* magazine rates the most popular tourist destinations in the world. To the early Chinese immigrants, it was the "Great City of the Golden Mountain." Because of its rapid and dramatic recovery from the 1906 Earthquake, it became known universally as "The city that knows how," a phrase originally credited to President William Howard Taft. Another president, Herbert Hoover, called it "the Athens of the United States," and Robert F. Kennedy once said that if he was elected president, he would move the White House here. Duke Ellington called it "one of the great cultural plateaus of the world," and James Michener called it "the most varied city in America." To many people, San Francisco was called "Frisco," a name that many residents despise. Most San Franciscans call it simply "the City," with a capital "C," a convention that we follow in this book. Perhaps Rudyard Kipling summed it up best when he said: "San Francisco has only one drawback. 'Tis hard to leave."

San Francisco's recorded history began in 1769, when its bay was discovered by Don Gaspar de Portola, leading a Spanish expedition up the coast. Native Americans had fished the waters of San Francisco Bay for centuries, but had apparently established no major settlement within what are now the city limits of San Francisco. Thus, the first permanent settlement was probably the establishment of a Spanish mission complex named for St. Francis of Assisi in 1776. The original Mission San Francisco de Asis still exists and is pictured on the following pages. The Spanish also established a fort—later the Presidio of San Francisco—overlooking the entrance to San Francisco Bay.

In 1822, with the Mexican Revolution, control of California passed from Spain to Mexico, but by that time, the population around San Francisco Bay was largely comprised of Americans who had come west to settle. In 1835, William Richardson founded the town of Yerba Buena (good herb) in what is now San Francisco's Financial District.

Dramatic changes transformed San Francisco in the 1840s. In 1846, California revolted against Mexican rule and declared itself a republic. A year later, Yerba Buena was officially renamed San Francisco. In 1848, an enormous gold discovery in the Sierra Nevada initiated the California Gold Rush of 1849. In 1850, California joined the United States and by 1852, San Francisco—as the gateway to the gold fields—had been transformed from a sleepy outpost into a world class metropolis.

Throughout the latter half of the nineteenth century, as money flowed out of the gold fields and in from international investors, San Francisco solidified its position as the preeminent city of the West. It had the grandest of houses and hotels, and a natural harbor unrivaled anywhere. It had truly become "The City at the End of the Rainbow."

On April 18, 1906, the City reached its turning point. At 5:12 that morning, the magnitude 8.3 Earthquake—always referred to in the City with a capital "E"—struck with all its fury. Between the Earthquake and the subsequent fires, most of San Francisco was destroyed. However, San Franciscans rebounded with amazing vigor, and the City was rebuilt, enlarged and improved within a few years. San Francisco then staged a world's fair, the 1915 Panama Pacific International Exposition, to celebrate.

This book is about where San Francisco has been, and how the City is today. Photographs of San Francisco as it is at the end of the twentieth century are compared with views of San Francisco as it was in years past, with those past years ranging from the 1850s to the 1950s. The pictures have each been selected for their ability to tell a particular story about a particular part of the City. In some areas of the City, the changes have been dramatic and the stories are dramatic. In others, the subtle changes also tell an interesting story. In some cases, we have even compared two historical photographs that tell the story of how certain parts of the City changed in the first decades after the Earthquake. While our primary focus is on famous vistas and familiar landmarks, we have also gone out to the neighborhoods, to look at the changes in the places where most San Franciscans live.

This is the story of San Francisco and its people and how they have molded this beautiful and picturesque place into one of the most visually exciting cities in the world.

Seen here in 1856 and dating back to 1776, Mission Dolores is the oldest building in San Francisco. It was founded by Father Junipero Serra as part of a series of missions a day's ride apart throughout California. It is officially the Mission of San Francisco de Asis (St. Francis of Assisi), but was nicknamed for the adjacent (now dry) Laguna de los Dolores (Lake of Our Lady of Sorrows).

Mission Dolores/San Francisco de Asis, as it appeared on Easter
Sunday in 1998. The City itself took its name from St. Francis of
Assisi, who is recognized as San Francisco's patron saint. The new
Mission Dolores Basilica to the right was built in 1918 and is an
integral part of San Francisco's Catholic community. It was the site
of a papal mass celebrated by John Paul II in 1987.

Downtown San Francisco—with San Francisco Bay beyond—as it appeared in 1905, a year before the Earthquake and fire. The photograph was actually taken from the top of Nob Hill between California Street and Pine Street. The Ferry Building tower is prominent on the waterfront, and Old St. Mary's Church can be seen on California Street below the Ferry Building.

The Ferry Building and Old St. Mary's are still landmarks in this
view of downtown San Francisco as it appeared in May 1947, but
the 11-year-old San Francisco-Oakland Bay Bridge dominates the
panorama. Among San Francisco's skyscrapers, the huge Russ Building
(*right*) was downtown's largest office tower from 1927, when it was
completed, through the 1950s.

This view looking east from the top of Nob Hill between Sacramento Street and California Street was taken in 1935 as the suspension cables were being strung for the San Francisco-Oakland Bay Bridge. Begun in 1933, the Bay Bridge opened in November 1936. The cable car tracks with the cable slot between them are clearly visible on California Street at the right.

The view looking east from the top of Nob Hill between Sacramento
Street and California Street as it appears today, shows how downtown
was transformed between the 1960s and the 1980s. Dominating the
Skyline today are the distinctive, 853-foot Transamerica Pyramid and
the 779-foot, black granite Bank of America World Headquarters.

This aerial view, taken looking east in the 1930s, captures the essence of downtown San Francisco as it was at the time. Most of the City's major buildings were between the massive Russ Building on Montgomery Street, between Pine Street and Bush Street, and the broad, diagonal thrust of Market Street (*right*). The waterfront was alive with tugs, ferries and other vessels.

When this aerial view was taken in the 1990s, the heart of San
Francisco's downtown Financial District—as it was now known—had
shifted several blocks to the north. The Russ Building (*right*) was now
dwarfed by the much taller skyscrapers built since the 1960s, especially
the imposing Bank of America World Headquarters. The waterfront
was now much quieter.

This 1939 aerial view looks southeast across downtown San Francisco toward the western anchorage of the San Francisco-Oakland Bay Bridge on Rincon Hill. At the time, both US Highway 40 and US Highway 50 crossed the bridge. At the center of this photograph, commuter rail lines from Oakland and beyond can be seen converging on the Transbay Terminal.

This contemporary aerial view looking southeast across downtown San Francisco toward the western anchorage of the San Francisco-Oakland Bay Bridge shows how much the City grew—vertically—in the latter half of the twentieth century. Also of note in this view are the number of pleasure craft sailing on San Francisco Bay.

Taken by an Army Air Corps pilot in April 1932, this photograph of the Embarcadero shows the area near the Ferry Building as a busy intersection point between the ferry dock on the left and the streetcar hub at the right. The even-numbered piers of the Port of San Francisco extend south toward where the Bay Bridge would be completed in 1936. Most of the piers in this picture have since been demolished.

The Embarcadero was revitalized early in the twenty-first century with landscaping and restored trolley lines. A broad promenade now extends from the Ferry Building south to the Bay Bridge. For three decades, the elevated double-decked Embarcadero Freeway cast its dark shadow across this scene, but it was pulled down after the 1989 Loma Prieta Earthquake to make way for the new look.

The San Francisco skyline as it appeared in 1916. The domed Call Building dominates the skyline at the left, while the Southern Pacific Building is under construction to the left of the Ferry Building. In the distance, the profiles of Twin Peaks, Mount Davidson and Golden Gate Heights can be seen.

The San Francisco skyline as it appeared in about 1939, looking west from Yerba Buena Island. Dramatic changes had occurred since the picture above was taken, with the construction of the Shell Oil Company Building (*to the left of the Ferry Building*) and the Russ Building (*to the right of the Ferry Building*). The Mark Hopkins Hotel can be seen atop Nob Hill to the right.

The San Francisco skyline as it appears today, looking west from Yerba Buena Island. The red-brick Southern Pacific Building (now part of One Market Plaza) is still visible, while the Ferry Building is now flanked to the right by the Hyatt Regency Hotel and the four similar towers of the Embarcadero Center. The green of Twin Peaks can be seen between the buildings.

This photograph, looking north from Nob Hill toward Russian Hill was taken in 1877 at a time when both hills were already crowded with a large number of substantial wood-frame houses. Clipper ships can be seen in San Francisco Bay between the City and Alcatraz Island, with Angel Island beyond. Alcatraz had been fortified by the US Army since 1859.

The view looking north from Nob Hill to Russian Hill as it appears today. The views from Russian Hill make it one of the City's more prestigious and popular residential areas. A large number of high-rise apartment buildings were constructed here from the 1930s through the 1960s. Height restrictions prohibit further such construction.

Seen here as it was in about 1940, Nob Hill was San Francisco's swank address. Like Russian Hill, it offered extraordinary views, but it was also just a short cable car's ride from the City's bustling downtown and retail district. The popular Mark Hopkins Hotel (*top of the hill, right*) was built on the site of the mansion of railroad baron Mark Hopkins, which was destroyed in 1906.

Nob Hill and adjacent areas as they appear today. The Mark Hopkins Hotel is still a prominent landmark, but it is now surrounded by a myriad of apartment buildings and dwarfed by the Transamerica Pyramid. To the right of the Mark Hopkins is the 32-story Fairmont Hotel Tower, whose base is also located on Nob Hill, 350 feet above the base of the Pyramid.

The view looking southeast from the top of Nob Hill after the Earthquake of April 18, 1906. Huge fires are burning at Third and Market streets (*top*), but the Nob Hill residents at the corner of Powell and Pine Streets (*bottom*) seem oblivious. Their homes are undamaged for now, but within three days, every wooden building on Nob Hill would burn to the ground.

The view looking southeast from the top of Nob Hill as it appears
today. After the 1906 disaster, Nob Hill was rebuilt using reinforced
masonry construction rather than wood. Because Nob Hill is bedrock,
wooden structures would survive an earthquake, but not another fire.
During the October 1989 earthquake, there was no major damage on
Nob Hill.

This dramatic photograph shows policemen patrolling Market Street near the base of O'Farrell Street shortly after the April 18, 1906 Earthquake. The damage caused by the Earthquake paled by comparison to the devastation caused by the 52 fires that burned through the City for several days. There were 315 people killed outright, and 28,000 buildings destroyed, most by fire.

The view looking east on Market Street from near O'Farrell Street as it appears today. The Call Building, named for *The Call* newspaper, was the City's tallest in 1906. It survived the Earthquake and became a symbol of the City's survival, but the dome was removed in the 1940s to modernize the structure. The newspaper soon folded and the building became The Central Tower.

When San Francisco blossomed into a metropolis at the time of the Gold Rush of 1849-1852, Market Street quickly evolved as San Francisco's main street. It was a broad, level boulevard with several cable car lines and all the best shops that led from the Ferry Building to the base of Twin Peaks. As seen here in 1908, the Call Building (*left*) was the dominant landmark.

By 1925, the horse and buggy era had faded into history and electric
streetcars had replaced cable cars on Market Street. In this elevated
view from the base of Powell Street, we see the domed Call Building,
which survived the 1906 Earthquake, and the domed Humboldt Bank
Building that was built shortly thereafter. The big Emporium
department store is at the right.

Since 1860, when the Market Street Railroad Company was formed, Market Street has been the focal point of San Francisco's transit corridors. As this 1937 photograph shows, the intersection of First Street was key bottleneck. It was here that streetcars made the turn toward the East Bay (now Transbay) Terminal for connections to Oakland and beyond.

Now in the deep shadows of the Financial District's concrete canyons, the corner of First and Market streets is still the turning point for the Transbay Terminal. Market Street is still the City's transit hub. On Market Street today, there are five electric subways, a surface electric streetcar line and a half dozen bus lines that reach out from here to all parts of San Francisco.

Located on the Embarcadero where Market Street meets San Francisco Bay, the Ferry Building was designed by Arthur Page Brown and opened in 1898 on the site of an 1875 wooden ferry house. With its 240-foot clock tower serving as a beacon, it was the portal to the City for anyone traveling from the north or east until the completion of the great bridges in 1936 and 1937.

Once the City's premier landmark, the Ferry Building survived the
Great Earthquake of 1906, but gradually fell into disuse in the 1950s.
Today, it once again serves as a ferry terminal. A major restoration
completed in 2003 has made it home to cafés, gourmet food shops, and
a weekly farmer's market. San Francisco's historic trolley cars pass its
doors on the Embarcadero.

The view looking east from the corner of Kearny and Market Streets in 1908, with the Ferry Building in the distance. Across the street on the right is the Palace Hotel, recently remodeled after the 1906 difficulties. Founded in 1875, the Palace was San Francisco's original "grand" hotel, with a reputation for being the finest and most luxurious hostelry west of Chicago.

The corner of Kearny and Market streets as it appears today. The Palace Hotel is now the Sheraton Palace and the cable cars on Kearny Street were long ago replaced by a bus line. Remodeled again in the 1990s, the Palace is no longer San Francisco's only grand hotel, but it still ranks among the best. President Warren G. Harding died here (some say he was poisoned) in 1923.

Right: Looking east on Geary Street toward Stockton Street on the morning of April 18, 1906, after the Earthquake, but before the fires swept through the area. Union Square is on the left, with some shrubbery barely visible. The Palace Hotel can be seen in the center at the intersection of Geary, Kearny and Market Streets. On the left, a couple in a motor car has apparently just driven down to survey what they don't yet know is the quiet before the storm. In the center, a pair of mounted policemen ride toward a crowd at Stockton Street.

Left: The view on Geary Street looking east toward Stockton Street in the spring of 1944. The lawns on the southeast corner of Union Square can be seen on the left. Sailors on liberty, who served aboard ships that had docked in San Francisco, were a common sight on the City's streets during World War II.

Above: As was the case in 1906 and in 1944, Union Square is the center of San Francisco's busy retail shopping district. While several of the buildings remain the same—some dating to before 1906—the businesses in them change constantly around Union Square. The Palace (now Sheraton Palace) Hotel remains at the end of the street. The palm trees were added after World War II.

In 1904, two years before the Earthquake, the Hotel St. Francis opened on Powell Street on the west side of Union Square. The square itself was named for the pro-Union rallies held here during the Civil War. The 90-foot column at the center of the square commemorates Admiral George Dewey's victory at Manila Bay in the Spanish-American War. The statue at the top is of Victory.

The view to the west across Union Square as it appears today. The third wing of what is now the Westin St. Francis Hotel was added after the Earthquake, and the 32-story St. Francis Tower was added in the 1960s. With 1,200 guest rooms, the hotel is one of the City's largest hotels. Cable cars still run on the Powell Street side of Union Square.

No.163-San Francisco rising from Ruins-April-18-1907.

Copyrighted 1907 by R. J. Waters & Co.

This photo, taken from Nob Hill on the first anniversary of the Great Earthquake of 1906, shows downtown San Francisco "rising from Ruins." Not so the great mansion of Southern Pacific Railroad general manager Alban Nelson Towne, located at 1101 California Street at Taylor Street. Only the grand portal remained, seen here in the center. The Masonic Auditorium now occupies this site.

Now known as the "Portals of the Past," the six marble Ionic columns
that once stood as the entrance to Alban Towne's palatial Nob Hill
mansion were moved to Golden Gate Park in 1909. They were
donated by Mrs. Towne to serve as a permanent rememberance of
the Earthquake. Here they remain, often overlooked, on the quiet
and serene shores of Lloyd Lake.

The cable car turntable at the base of Powell Street on a rainy March day in 1945. Another cable car can be seen coming down Nob Hill in the distance. Located at Market Street, three blocks from Union Square, this turntable was one of many in the City in 1945, and one of three that survive today. The California Street line uses double-ended cars that need not be turned around.

In 1945, the cable car turntable at the foot of Powell Street was just an ordinary, everyday part of the City's Municipal Railway transit system. Today, as seen here, it is one of the City's chief tourist attractions, as people queue up for a ride. Two of the City's three surviving cable car lines—the Powell-Hyde and Powell-Mason—have their terminus here.

Also taken in March 1945, this photograph is the reverse of the one on page 42. Here, the view is down Powell Street toward Union Square, and to the foot of Powell Street at Market Street. The tall building on the left is the Art Deco style Sir Francis Drake Hotel. The star at the top of the building denotes the Starlight Roof, which was one of the City's swankest night spots in the 1940s.

Today, the view down Powell Street from between California Street and Pine Street is much as it was a half century ago. Indeed, the same cable cars which were already old in 1945, are still in service today. A full-time Municipal Railway maintenance department cares for them meticulously, however. The Sir Francis Drake is still there, although it is now hidden by the Holiday Inn tower.

Though San Francisco is well known for its cable cars, the City once had the most comprehensive system of electric trolleys west of the Mississippi. It was operated by the privately owned Market Street Railway Company and by the City's Municipal Railway. Here is the Market Street Railway's southbound Number 27 Bryant car on Second Street near Howard Street in 1939.

The great thing about this twenty-first-century view of Second Street
near Howard Street is that the row of buildings on the east side of the
street is virtually unchanged in seven decades! The electric trolley lines
were pulled out long ago, and Second Street is now served by the San
Francisco Municipal Railway's Number 10 and Number 15 diesel buses.

The view looking southeast across Nob Hill from the corner of Clay Street and Jones Street after the April 18, 1906 Earthquake and firestorm swept the area. Only the Fairmont Hotel and the 1885 brownstone mansion of James Flood survived of the buildings atop the hill. Made of wood, the other grand homes burned to the ground. The Call Building can be seen in the distance.

The Fairmont Hotel and the Flood mansion (now the Pacific-Union Club) as seen from Sacramento Street near Jones Street today. Because of rebuilding that has occurred since 1906, the only two "pre-Earthquake" buildings on Nob Hill are no longer visible from Clay Street. The Pacific-Union Club bought the gutted brownstone in 1907 and spent over three years remodeling it.

In July 1905, lower California Street had been second only to Market Street among San Francisco's important commercial streets for half a century. In the early days, the cable car lines were owned by individual companies. The California Street firm had been one of the first to tackle the City's daunting hills. Now part of the Municipal Railway, the California Street cars still operate.

The view down California Street from Kearny Street as it appears today. Note that the building at the corner of Montgomery Street a block down on the left appears in both pictures. It survived the 1906 Earthquake and a century of downtown modernization. Many of the masonry buildings in this area survived the Earthquake, only to be gutted by fire. Most of these were restored in 1906.

This rooftop view looking westward up California Street, toward the top of Nob Hill, was taken from between Montgomery Street and Kearny Street, in 1905, a year before the Earthquake and fires wrought their devastation here. The Fairmont Hotel, at the top on the left, was nearing completion. Old St. Mary's Church, built in 1854, is seen just beneath the Fairmont.

The view up California Street toward the top of Nob Hill, as it
appeared in about 1925. Many masonry, but no wood, structures
survived the 1906 disaster. Burned, but left structurally intact, the
Fairmont Hotel soon remodeled and opened. The pagoda-style Trade
Mark Building across Grant Avenue from Old St. Mary's identifies
the street as being part of Chinatown (*see pages 68-69*).

Looking east at Sansome Street, toward the Southern Pacific Building at the foot of California Street. This photo was taken in 1941, before World War II-gas rationing took many cars off the streets. The cable slots are clearly visible between the cable car tracks. A cable car moves by reaching into the slot and gripping a long, continuous, moving cable that runs the length of the street.

Looking east at Sansome Street toward the foot of California Street.
The Southern Pacific Building is now part of the One Market Plaza
complex, and San Francisco's once-proud Southern Pacific Railroad
became part of long-time rival Union Pacific in 1995. The Union Bank
(no relation) Building (*left*) replaced the old Alaska Commercial
Building in 1977.

Looking west on California Street from the corner of Kearny Street in 1880. Completed in 1854, Old St. Mary's was then St. Mary's Cathedral, the seat of the Catholic Archdiocese of San Francisco, which encompassed much of California, as well as Nevada and Utah. The California House was one of the City's favorite eateries, noted for "fresh oysters in every style."

The view of California Street from Kearny Street as it appears today. Old
St. Mary's still stands. It ceased to be the cathedral in 1891, when "New"
St. Mary's was built across town on Geary Street. "New" St. Mary's
burned in 1962 and was replaced by a third St. Mary's. The site of the
California House now contains the 33-story Hartford Insurance Building.

The view looking west on California Street from Front Street, on a hazy day in about 1925. By this time, automobiles had completely replaced horses on the streets of San Francisco. The streets were cleaner, but the air was not. Many of these buildings housed high-flying stock brokerage firms that would suffer in the impending Stock Market Crash of 1929.

Looking west on California Street from Front Street today. Many of the
same buildings between Front Street and Battery Street are still here,
although past Battery Street to the west, new construction has replaced
many of the buildings that were in place in the 1920s. The Tadich
Grill, which dates from 1849, was originally on nearby Clay Street.

The view from Powell Street up toward the crest of Nob Hill as it
appeared in 1929. On the left are the Stanford Court Apartments (later
Hotel) and the Mark Hopkins Hotel. These hotels were built on the
sites of the mansions of Central Pacific and Southern Pacific Railroad
founders Leland Stanford and Mark Hopkins. Both homes burned in
the 1906 fires. The Fairmont Hotel is on the right.

The view up the last inclined block of California Street before the top
of Nob Hill as it appears today. The south tower of Grace Cathedral
can be seen on the top of the hill on the right, dwarfed by the massive
luxury apartment building at the corner of California Street and Jones
Street. The Fairmont Hotel still takes up the entirety of the right side
of the street.

The view looking east on California Street from Powell Street, seen here in the 1940s, has always been one of San Francisco's more dramatic street-level panoramas. The Southern Pacific Building is at the base of the street, with the 519-foot West Tower of the San Francisco-Oakland Bay Bridge behind it. The Oakland Hills and Mount Diablo are visible in the far distance.

Looking east on California Street from Powell Street is still a spectacular vista. The San Francisco-Oakland Bay Bridge is still visible, but newer buildings now block much of the view beyond. On the left is the massive Hartford Insurance Building, while on the right are the International Building and the black granite Bank of America World Headquarters.

A group consisting primarily of downtown office workers aboard the California Street cable car as it passes in front of the Mark Hopkins Hotel near the top of Nob Hill, circa 1945. While today cable cars are thought of primarily as entertainment for tourists, in the 1940s, they were still an important means of transportation for commuters.

The California Street cable car passing near the Mark Hopkins Hotel—now the Mark Hopkins Intercontinental—in 1998. By the 1950s, the tracks on this line had been eliminated between Van Ness Avenue and Presidio Avenue. This truncation of the route reduced its usefulness to San Franciscans, but the line still has a lower proportion of tourists than the other two lines.

California St.   East from Polk Street   194_

The view to the east on California Street from Polk Street in 1944. The street is named for President James K. Polk—who never visited San Francisco—but some wish it were named for San Francisco architect Willis Polk, who designed many important City buildings, such as the Merchants' Exchange on California Street (1903) and the Hallidie Building on Sutter Street (1917).

The corner of Polk and California Streets as it appears today. Polk Gulch is one of many neighborhoods where changes have been relatively slow in the latter part of the twentieth century, although American Trust is now The Gap. The top of Nob Hill, seen in the distance, however, saw the construction of many luxury high-rise apartment buildings.

The view looking north from California Street into Grant Avenue, the "main street" of San Francisco's Chinatown, in about 1928. Originally known as Dupont Street, Grant Avenue was called Du Baan Gai or "street of the slatboard capital city" by the Chinese. It was renamed at the time of the Civil War for General Ulysses S. Grant. The first Chinese to come to live in San Francisco arrived in 1848 and 1849 at the time of the Gold Rush, and soon the area around Grant Avenue was filled with Chinese shops and businesses. The Chinese term for what is now Chinatown was Ton Yen Fau, or Port of the Chinese. San Francisco itself was the Golden Mountain.

Looking north from California Street into Grant Avenue today. The Trade Mark Building, with its emblem of eight trigrams, has been a familiar Chinatown landmark since it was built shortly after the 1906 Earthquake, although the tenants have changed through the years. Until as late as the 1970s, Grant Avenue was a street of almost exclusively Chinese shops. However, in recent years, the parts of the street closest to California Street have come to be dominated primarily by businesses that cater to tourists. Neighboring Stockton Street and various side streets have become the "real" Chinatown, with Chinese stores and many popular Chinese restaurants.

Looking north on Grant Avenue from near Vinton Alley in 1932. The notorious Shanghai Low was one of the more popular nightclubs in San Francisco during the 1930s and 1940s. Its clientele included Chinese and non-Chinese alike, with the latter coming to the Shanghai Low to experience a culture that was still considered "exotic" by many European Americans.

The view on Grant Avenue from near Vinton Alley as it appears today. All of the buildings that were here in 1932 still remain, but all of the businesses have changed, primarily to shops selling jewelry and Chinese arts and crafts to visitors. The building that once housed the legendary Shanghai Low is now home to the Lotus Garden, a vegetarian restaurant.

Seen here circa 1850, with Telegraph Hill beyond, Portsmouth Square at Clay and Kearny streets was San Francisco's original downtown. In July 1846, Captain John Montgomery of the USS Portsmouth first raised an American flag over San Francisco on this spot. Saloons and gambling halls once surrounded the square, but so too did the City's first important banks and commercial enterprises. In 1847, the first public school in California opened in Portsmouth Square, and the San Francisco Hall of Justice was located here until 1961.

Today, the line of buildings seen on the opposite (north) side of Portsmouth Square rose after the 1906 Earthquake from the same foundations as the buildings seen in the previous image. Coit Tower, seen here at right, marks the top of Telegraph Hill, which is largely barren in the opposite view. The square is the heart of Chinatown, but the commercial core of San Francisco is just a short walk from here. Many historically important California companies, such as Wells Fargo Bank, still have their headquarters nearby.

The dream of millionaire developer Adolph Sutro, the Sutro Baths opened in 1896. It was the world's largest bathhouse, containing no less than seven swimming pools, and it encompassed three acres on the Pacific shore near the Cliff House. The Sutro Baths could accommodate 10,000 people at one time—and often did. Stage shows were presented at a 3,700-seat amphitheater, and there were three restaurants to cater to its patrons.

The Sutro Baths remained an important part of life for San Franciscans
for more than a generation, but its popularity waned by the time of
World War II. Plans were underway to replace the bathhouse with
high-rise apartments when the complex was destroyed in a devastating
1966 fire. The ruins became part of the Golden Gate National
Recreation Area in 1973.

The view across the Golden Gate in the summer of 1934, as work was just beginning on the south tower. The brick structure at the edge of the water is the US Army's Fort Point, located on the point of land also known as Fort Point. It was completed in 1861, before the Civil War. It was intended to help defend San Francisco Bay, but it was abandoned as obsolete in 1900.

The view across the Golden Gate toward Marin Headland as it appears today. The bridge was designed by Joseph Strauss, with structural engineering work done by Charles Ellis and Leon Moisseiff. The 1861 fort is still present on Fort Point, having survived a 1930s proposal that it be torn down during the bridge's construction. It is now under the jurisdiction of the National Park Service and is a National Historic Site.

The Golden Gate Bridge as it appeared late in 1936, with the cables strung and large segments of the roadway in place. The roadway was finally in place by April 1937 and the bridge opened with Pedestrian Day on May 27. The next Pedestrian Day would be on May 27, 1987, on the 50th anniversary. It took 25 million man-hours to build, but only 11 people were killed in accidents.

The Golden Gate Bridge as it appears today from the road leading to
Fort Point. The first year that the bridge was open, it carried 3.5
million vehicles. Today, the annual totals average close to 40 million. It
cost $35 million to build, with the construction bonds being paid off in
1971. The replacement cost is estimated to be about $1.3 billion.

This aerial view of the Golden Gate Bridge was taken in early 1935 from high over the Marin Headlands, looking south into San Francisco. The north (nearer) tower is complete, and work is still continuing on the south tower. The Parade Grounds of the US Army's Presidio of San Francisco are visible to the left of the south tower. Beyond the wooded hills of the Presidio are the streets and houses of the Richmond District and the Sunset District. Between them, the dark, horizontal band is Golden Gate Park.

This aerial view of the Golden Gate Bridge was taken in August 1995, looking north across the Marin Headlands. US Highway 101 and California Highway 1 are contiguous as they cross the bridge and climb the Waldo Grade. The towers each stand 746 feet above the water of the Golden Gate, the channel that leads from the Pacific Ocean into San Francisco Bay. The center span of the bridge—once the longest in the world—is 4,200 feet long and 220 feet above the water. The bridge itself is 6,450 feet in length and 90 feet wide.

This photograph of the San Francisco-Oakland Bay Bridge was taken from Yerba Buena Island in 1954, when there was still two-way traffic on the top deck and the Key System inter-urban railway cars running on the bottom. The City's skyline was dominated by the Pacific Telephone Building (*left*), the Russ Building (*center*) and the Mark Hopkins Hotel (*right*) on Nob Hill.

Today the traffic on the San Francisco-Oakland Bay Bridge is inbound on the top deck and outbound on the bottom. The rail cars are long gone, although there are always suggestions that they be brought back. Seen here, the suspension section of the bridge is 6,940 feet long. One small section of the upper deck broke loose in the 1989 earthquake, but it was repaired in 30 days.

Part of San Francisco's mystique has always been its reputation for wild, "anything goes" night life, but this has usually been confined to specific districts. For many years it was in the area between downtown and Telegraph Hill, known as the Barbary Coast. In the 1940s and 1950s, one notorious block of Pacific Avenue set itself apart as "the International Settlement."

Today, the bawdy "International Settlement" (which was neither international nor a settlement) has disappeared without a trace, its wild night life just a hazy figment of the fading memories of the sailors and travelling salesmen who experienced its naughtiness. This block of Pacific Avenue (formerly Pacific Street) has been incorporated back into Jackson Square.

North Beach was the focal point of Italian immigration in the nineteenth century that included the people who created San Francisco's once famous fishing fleet. It evolved as a neighborhood to include the shore of San Francisco Bay at the City's northeast corner and the area west of Telegraph Hill. Columbus Avenue, seen here in 1945, was its main street.

The view today, looking north as Columbus Avenue crosses Filbert Street and Powell Street. North Beach still celebrates its Italian heritage with the annual Columbus Day parade. While many of the Italian shops that survived here as late as the 1970s are gone, the district still boasts a myriad of great Italian delicatessens, restaurants and espresso bars.

The view looking south on Columbus Avenue at Vallejo Street as it appeared in August 1944. The building at the base of the street is the famous Montgomery Block, known as "the Monkey Block," which was famous at the time for containing the studios of artists, illustrators, writers and "Bohemians," all of whom liked the proximity to the espresso and good pasta of North Beach.

Today, the view looking south on Columbus Avenue at Vallejo Street is dominated by the skyscrapers built between the 1960s and the 1980s. "The Monkey Block" was demolished in order to build the Transamerica Pyramid. Completed in 1972, the Pyramid dwarfs the green-domed Victorian Columbus Tower Building that was a Columbus Avenue landmark since the Earthquake.

In 1877, when this panorama of Telegraph Hill was taken from Nob Hill, both hills and the City below were already densely populated and filled with many substantial commercial buildings. Through the nineteenth century, the San Francisco waterfront was always crowded with the big clipper ships that brought people here from around Cape Horn or from the Orient.

Today, Telegraph Hill is dominated by 210-foot Coit Tower, completed in
1933 and named for Lillie Hitchcock Coit, who funded its construction
to commemorate the volunteer firemen of the City, especially those who
fought the fires in 1906. It is supposed to resemble a fire hose nozzle.
Columbus Avenue runs horizontally through the center of these pictures.

In the 1920s, before the construction of Coit Tower, the top of Telegraph Hill was still a dusty, out-of-the-way working class neighborhood. While Nob Hill and Russian Hill had mansions, paved streets and cable cars, the views from Telegraph Hill had not yet been "discovered." The hill was named, not for telegraph poles, but for a semaphore that signaled ship arrivals.

Today, the view looking east from the corner of Montgomery and Union streets is recognized as one of San Francisco's most spectacular. The steep streets of Telegraph Hill—which long stifled residential development, and which still frighten drivers from flatland areas—are now considered to be an important part of the charm of life on Telegraph Hill.

Frederick Layman's legendary Old German Castle sits atop Telegraph Hill, as viewed from Green Street on Russian Hill in about 1895. In 1906, fires destroyed everything seen here, except the castle, which had burned in 1903. Built in 1882, "Layman's Folly" was intended to be a fashionable resort, but after a fatal wreck on Layman's private cable car line, business went downhill.

Today, the view of Telegraph Hill from Green Street on Russian Hill includes the numerous apartment houses that now crowd both hills. Many of these, especially the three in the middle of this picture, were built immediately after the 1906 Earthquake. These two hills, North Beach (which lies between them) and neighboring Chinatown are the City's most densely populated areas.

More a mountain road than a boulevard, Telegraph Hill Boulevard is actually an extension of Lombard Street. It is seen here shortly after it officially opened in 1933 as the access road to the newly-completed Coit Tower. Some of the best views in San Francisco can be had from the apartment houses that were built on Telegraph Hill Boulevard, but Coit Tower traffic is a nuisance.

Looking northwest from the slopes of Telegraph Hill just beneath
Coit Tower, one can see Alcatraz in the distance. Between 1934 and
1963, federal prisoners on "the Rock" watched the lights of these
apartment houses on Telegraph Hill longingly. The lights were so
near (1.5 miles), but so far. There were no known, successful escape
attempts from Alcatraz.

This 1922 photograph shows construction work on Lombard Street between Hyde and Leavenworth streets. Rather than simply paving the street, the City chose to use eight switchbacks to overcome the 27 percent slope of this block. There are four conventionally paved blocks in the City that are steeper, with one on Filbert Street and one on 22nd Street having 31.5 percent grades.

This contemporary photograph looking up Lombard was taken early on a Sunday morning before the the lines of tourists had arrived to drive its famous twists and turns. Billed as "the Crookedest Street in the World," this block of Lombard Street is actually the City's second crookedest. Vermont Street between McKinley and 22nd streets has much sharper turns.

In this 1939 view looking up Market Street from the top of Twin Peaks, one can make out the buildings of the Golden Gate International Exposition on Treasure Island at the top left. This world's fair, held concurrently with one in New York, was actually two fairs, one held in 1939 and another on the same site in 1940. Treasure Island is actually an artificial island created to host the fair.

The popular view down Market Street from Twin Peaks is still the highest panorama of San Francisco that one can drive to. The City's skyline now blocks much of the view of 400-acre Treasure Island. The Golden Gate International Exposition was demolished in 1940, and the island served as a US Navy base from World War II until the 1990s.

Already the site of many fine homes, Pacific Heights emerged after the 1906 Earthquake and fire as the City's most exclusive residential district. The burned out top of Nob Hill, with the forlorn Fairmont Hotel, can be seen in the distance. These homes on Gough Street survived because Van Ness Avenue, two blocks east, was used as a firebreak to stop the progress of the fire.

These two Queen Anne Victorian homes on Gough Street (*seen opposite*) survived the Earthquake and fire in 1906 and have each celebrated their 100th anniversary. In the background, later construction on Nob Hill has replaced the damaged buildings, and has eliminated the view of the Fairmont. Both of these pictures were taken from a hill in Lafayette Park.

This photograph of Pier 39 was taken in December 1953, during a labor action against the Blue Star Line. Early in the twentieth century, most of San Francisco's piers were configured with distinctive, uniform facades, such as seen here. As the port went into decline in the 1950s, and the piers fell into disuse, the facades were torn down. Only a handful of them remain.

Pier 39 as it appears today is a far cry from its days as a working maritime wharf. Since 1978, when it was opened in its present form by developer Warren Simmons, it has become one of the City's foremost tourist venues, with a myriad of shops and eating places. San Francisco piers were given sequential odd numbers north of the Ferry Building, and even numbers to the south.

Right: Fishing boats tied up on the docks adjacent to Jefferson Street between Jones and Powell streets in 1928. Large-scale commercial fishing, which began with the Italian immigrants in the nineteenth century, was to be a major industry in this area for many years.

Left: Fishing boats tied up on the docks adjacent to Jefferson Street between Jones and Powell streets, circa 1950. The complex of docks between this point and Pier 45 (*far left*), as well as Pier 47 (*out of the picture to the left*), are what constitute the area familiarly known as Fisherman's Wharf. Large seafood restaurants catering to tourists first started to open in the area in the 1930s.

Above: Today, there are still boats tied up on the docks adjacent to
Jefferson Street between Jones and Powell Streets, with many doing
charter fishing as well as commercial fishing. The three restaurants seen
here have been on "the Wharf" for over half a century. A member of
the Alioto family, Joseph Lawrence "Joe" Alioto, served as Mayor of
San Francisco from 1967 through 1975.

Right: Looking west through the western part of the Fisherman's Wharf area, with Pier 47 on the right. Missing in the distance from this 1925 photograph, but seen in the other two pictures, is the Golden Gate Bridge, which would not be completed for another decade.

Left: Looking west toward the Golden Gate Bridge, circa 1940. More than 80 kinds of fish and shellfish are landed in San Francisco area harbors each year. The three most economically important species have traditionally been salmon, Pacific herring, and Dungeness crab. Together, these three species account for about half of the total catch.

Above: The view looking west toward the Golden Gate Bridge, with Pier 47 on the right, as it appears today. Chinook or king salmon have supported a commercial fishery in and around San Francisco Bay since the mid-nineteenth century. Recently, the commercial catch of salmon had an average annual value of nearly $9 million.

Watching commercial fishermen at work in a fishing boat outside the Fishermen's Grotto Restaurant in 1939. Note the Golden Gate International Exposition flag flying beneath the sign. The Pacific herring has also been an important commercial species in San Francisco Bay since the nineteenth century. In 1892, more than four million pounds were caught, and in 1980, the 17 million pounds that were landed in San Francisco had a value of $16 million.

A contemporary photograph of fishing boats tied outside the Fishermen's Grotto Restaurant. Dungeness crab has always been a popular item with visitors to "the Wharf." Although the annual harvest earlier in this century was generally around three million pounds, recent harvests have been less than one-third of this level. Nevertheless, in recent years, San Francisco Bay Area crab landings have been valued at more than $1 million. Since 1900, all harvest of Dungeness crab has been outside the Bay.

The Palace of Fine Arts under construction in 1915. The neoclassical structure was designed by legendary architect Bernard Maybeck as one of the important pavilions of the Panama Pacific International Exposition that was staged by San Francisco in 1925 to celebrate the City's recovery from the 1906 Earthquake and its emergence as a world-class city.

The Palace of Fine Arts as it appears today. Intended to be torn down at the end of the Panama Pacific International Exposition, it was built of wood and plaster as a temporary structure. The palace was spared, but it deteriorated terribly until it was rebuilt in 1962 using concrete. Since 1969 it has housed the Exploratorium, a world-famous, hands-on science museum.

This view looking west toward Twin Peaks from upper Eureka Valley
dates from the early 1930s, and many of the homes seen here date from
the Victorian era. In the twenty-first century, the character of the quiet
residential neighborhoods of Eureka Valley and neighboring Noe Valley
remains little changed. The hills provide varied and interesting vistas.

A major change in the hills and valleys east of Twin Peaks is the notable increase in the number of trees, while a building boom in the 1950s and 1960s added a great many homes to the slopes of the Twin Peaks themselves. The 977-foot Sutro Tower entered service in 1973, sending television signals into the nooks and crannies of San Francisco's steep terrain.

Looking east toward downtown from Alamo Square, near the center of the City sometime before 1906. The dome of San Francisco's City Hall can be seen at the right. Built in 1895, this building was destroyed in the 1906 Earthquake. The reason was faulty concrete that escaped the watchful eye of City inspectors. The wooden Victorian houses would survive the Earthquake.

The view to the east from Alamo Square as it appears today, about 20
feet from where the facing page picture was taken. Most of the Victorian
houses around the square still stand after more than a century. The park
itself was laid out in the 1860s and named with the Spanish word for
poplar. Considered quite fashionable in the 1890s, Alamo Square is now
a middle class neighborhood.

Looking west on Haight Street past Clayton Street toward Golden Gate Park on a rainy winter day in 1944. The Haight Ashbury evolved in the Victorian era essentially as a suburb, away from downtown, but still within commuting distance. A middle class neighborhood in the 1940s, it declined in the 1950s and was discovered in the 1960s because of low rents and Victorian charm.

Haight Street between Ashbury and Clayton streets as it appears today. From 1965 to 1968, Haight Street was the epicenter of a counterculture that was invented here and presented to the world in the 1967 "Summer of Love." After decades of deterioration, Haight Street is now reemerging as a popular restaurant street. Shops still purvey Summer of Love memorabilia to curious tourists.

There were still relatively few cars on the streets of San Francisco when this photograph was taken, looking north on Church Street from near the top of Dolores Heights in about 1930. Dolores Park can be seen at the right, with Mission High School visible across the park on 18th Street. Mission Dolores, for which the park is named, is two blocks north of the school.

Looking north on Dolores Street from just above 20th Street today.
This view would still be recognized by a visitor from 1930, although
there are now trees along the western edge of Dolores Park, Mission
High School has changed and there are more cars. The J-Line streetcar
tracks still run through the park parallel to Church Street.

Right: Looking north on Church Street from the corner of 22nd Street at the base of Dolores Heights. This photograph was taken in July 1916 at a time when many streets in the area remained unpaved. The J-Line streetcar tracks can be seen winding to the right to bypass the steepest part of the hill. They rejoin Church Street at 18th Street.

Left: Looking south at 18th Street and the base of Dolores Heights, with an unpaved Church Street on the right. This photograph was taken as the J-Line streetcar tracks were under construction through the western edge of Dolores Park.

Left: The view up Church Street from the corner of 22nd Street at the base of Dolores Heights as it appears today. The J-Line streetcar still runs on this route, and it still runs through a series of backyards to avoid the top of the hill. Across the hill, the tracks parallel Church Street, which forms the western boundary of Dolores Park.

Right: The view looking south at 18th Street and the base of Dolores Heights today. Church Street has long since been paved and the J-Line streetcars still make their run across Dolores Heights through the western edge of Dolores Park.

The vast Richmond District comprises the western half of San Francisco north of Golden Gate Park and is one of the City's largest districts. Geary Boulevard, seen here in March 1944, was—and still is—the Richmond's busiest and most important thoroughfare. The Alexandria, a movie palace in the Art Deco style was—and still is—an important entertainment venue.

Geary Boulevard at 19th Avenue as it appears today. While Will King
poured his last kup of koffee many years ago, the Alexandria is still
going strong, with Academy Award-winning fare. Today, the Richmond
District is an ethnically diverse area, with large, first-generation
Chinese, Russian, Middle Eastern and Irish populations.

Looking south from Red Rock Hill along four-lane Diamond Heights Boulevard in 1963, with Duncan Street crossing in the foreground. Largely devoid of trees, the rolling hills of Diamond Heights were the last large open space to be developed in San Francisco. Because of zoning and other restrictions, this will be the last such development in the City.

The view from Red Rock Hill looking toward the Diamond Heights Shopping Center as it appears today. The housing in this area was constructed rapidly during a relatively short span of time. The architecture of San Francisco's "newest neighborhood" reflects the Bauhaus-inspired "boxiness" that was in fashion during the 1960s and early 1970s, when the area was being built.

An L-Line streetcar emerges from the West Portal of the Twin Peaks Tunnel, then known as Claremont Station, at the time of its first use by streetcars in February 1918. Built between 1914 and 1917 and originally used by automobiles, the Twin Peaks Tunnel changed the history of San Francisco dramatically by linking its downtown to its virtually unpopulated western half.

A contemporary photograph of an L-Line streetcar emerging from
the West Portal of the Twin Peaks Tunnel. The flamboyant covering
that obscures the wonderful old beaux-arts portal arch was designed
and constructed in the 1970s at the time that the San Francisco
Municipal Railway acquired the Boeing Vertol rail cars such as we
find pictured here.

Climbing out of Noe Valley, the Castro Street Cable Car crosses 23rd Street heading north, circa 1939. A prosperous middle class neighborhood since it was developed as a residential area in the 1880s, Noe Valley was originally the San Miguel Rancho, owned by Jose Jesus de Noe, who served as the last Mexican alcalde (mayor) of San Francisco.

The view into Noe Valley at 23rd Street as it appears today. Still a
bustling middle class neighborhood, Noe Valley is served by several
bus lines but no cable cars. By 1957, San Francisco had systematically
eliminated all but three of its more than 20 cable car lines. The last
three were saved when it was discovered that both residents and
visitors enjoyed riding on cable cars.

The view on 24th Street at Diamond Street, looking west toward Twin Peaks in June 1909. Even as 24th Street was evolving as Noe Valley's commercial center, the slopes of Twin Peaks were still being used to graze livestock, much as when Jose de Jesus Noe maintained his ranch on this land. The "Peaks" are a pair of virtually identical knolls, 903 and 910 feet high.

The corner of 24th Street and Diamond as it appears today. With the exception of conveniences such as cars and cappuccino, the overall feel of Noe Valley is generally as it was before, but rapid development of multi-unit buildings in the 1950s dramatically altered the slopes of Twin Peaks. The uppermost parts of both hills are now, however, preserved from further development.

Looking east on 24th Street toward Noe Street on a rainy December day in 1944. Noe Valley's commercial "main street" was then being served by an electric street car line. Such vehicles are distinguished from cable cars by the overhead electric wires and the absence of a cable slot between the two rails. Today, 24th Street has a cross-town bus line.

The center of Noe Valley, 24th Street is still a convenient shopping
street at the heart of a close-knit family neighborhood that prides itself
on a "small town within the City" atmosphere. Though many business
names have changed, a person who grew up here in the 1890s or 1940s
would recognize most of the buildings.

Shotwell Street, seen here looking north from 26th Street, was traditionally one of the Mission District's more important residential areas. Immediately after the 1906 Earthquake, however, many Shotwell Street residents moved to makeshift housing in the middle of the street until their houses were repaired from quake-related damage.

Shotwell Street between 25th Street and 26th Street is still a
comfortable residential neighborhood that has obviously benefitted
by the maturing of its street trees. It is typical of the streets throughout
the city where pre-1906 Victorian architecture survived both the
Earthquake and fires of 1906 and the "modernization" madness of
the 1950s.

The Sunset District in January 1940, looking down Quintara Street from just above 15th Avenue, past the Lincoln High School construction site to the Pacific Ocean. The area, which stretches from Twin Peaks to the Pacific Ocean, was nothing but sand dunes in 1920, and some patches of sand are still visible in this picture.

The sprawling Sunset District as it appears today from Quintara Street and 15th Avenue. For a half century, the Sunset has been the City's largest district. Although the eastern edge of the Sunset is a few miles from the Civic Center, it was effectively cut off from the rest of the city until completion of the Twin Peaks Tunnel and the improvement of Portola Drive across the Peaks.

Right: The front entrance to the main midway of Playland-At-The-Beach, as it appeared in the early 1950s. For anyone who grew up in San Francisco during most of the twentieth century, Playland-At-The-Beach was an essential part of life. With rides, games, snack bars and amusements, Playland-At-The-Beach was San Francisco's Coney Island.

Left: The famous Big Dipper Roller Coaster at the end of Fulton Street was the essential landmark at Playland-At-The-Beach. It opened in 1922, and was, for many years, the largest roller coaster west of the Mississippi.

Left: Where Playland-At-The-Beach once stood, there is now a group of apartment complexes. Playland-At-The-Beach first opened in 1916, directly across The Great Highway from the Pacific Ocean, between Fulton Street and Balboa Street. George Whitney bought it in 1928 and expanded it to 10 acres.

Right: On Fulton Street where the Big Dipper once stood, there is now an apartment house, but for many years after Playland-At-The-Beach was destroyed, the vast site remained as just an empty field of drifting sand.

Above: The classic view of the Cliff House in about 1901. Located overlooking the Pacific Ocean on Land's End, the westernmost promontory of San Francisco, the Cliff House was the City's Shangri-la. The first Cliff House was built on this site in 1863 and purchased in 1881 by multi-millionaire silver baron and (briefly) mayor of San Francisco, Adolph Sutro. After a fire in 1894, Sutro rebuilt the Cliff House in French Chateau style, as seen here. It had an observation tower two hundred feet above sea level, parlors with panoramic views from large windows, a large art gallery, a large public dining room, a grand parlor, a bar, numerous private dining rooms and kitchens. This was the most resplendent and beloved of all the Cliff Houses, but it was the shortest lived.

Left: Having survived the 1906 Earthquake and fire by being built on rock and being five miles from the nearest major fire, Adolph Sutro's splendid second Cliff House went up in smoke in September 1907.

Above: The third and present Cliff House was constructed on the
site in 1909 by Sutro's daughter Emma. It continued to serve as a
restaurant, although it never matched the grandeur of its predecessor.
In 1952, the Sutro family sold it to George Whitney. It was remodeled
several times before the National Park Service acquired it in 1977 as
part of the Golden Gate National Recreation Area.

INDEX